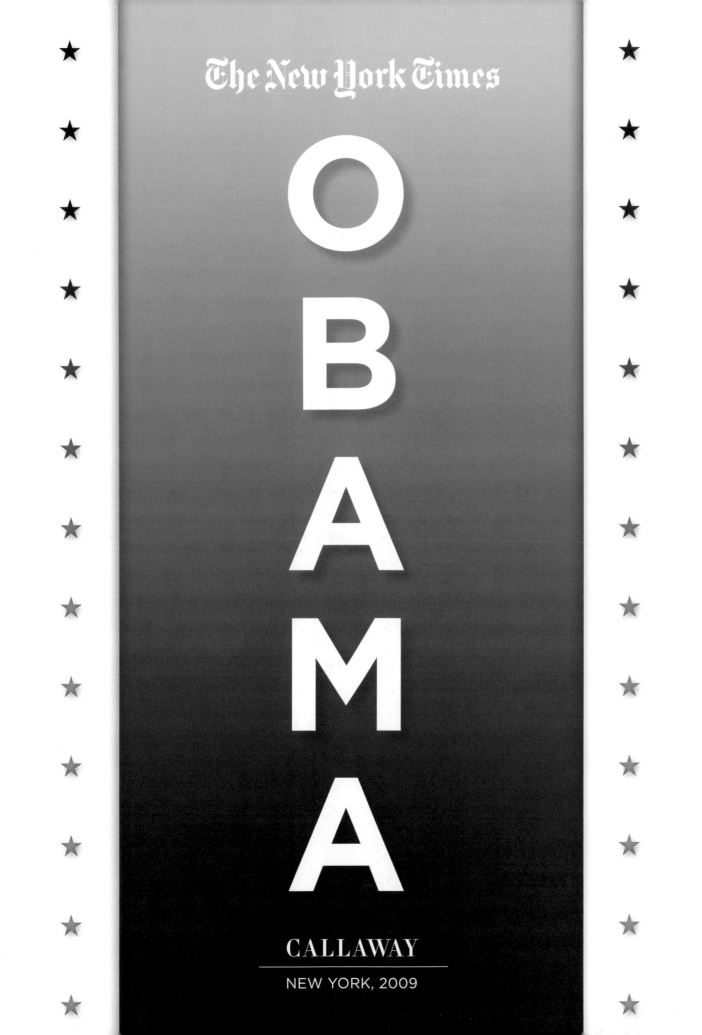

The New York Times

OBAMA

CALLAWAY

NEW YORK, 2009

Senator Barack Obama at a rally in Jacksonville, Fla. September 20, 2008.

The candidate speaking in a heavy rain at a rally,
Widener University, Chester, Pa. October 28, 2008.

Senator Barack Obama at a press conference following a town hall meeting with veterans in San Antonio, Tex. March 3, 2008.

YOUNG READER'S EDITION

OBAMA

THE HISTORIC JOURNEY

TEXT BY JILL ABRAMSON

DESIGN BY KRUPA JHAVERI

The New York Times

CALLAWAY

NEW YORK

2009

contents

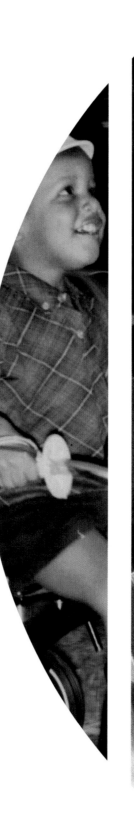

DAMON WINTER/NYT

WINDS
OF CHANGE

Across the country, on Nov. 4, 2008, voting lines were longer than anyone could remember. For thousands of Americans, an activity that usually took 15 minutes stretched into hours of waiting. But the moods near polling places were light; most people were excited and willing to wait to cast their vote in this historic election.

In Albany, Ga., 67-year-old Rutha Mae Harris was among the foot soldiers of the civil rights movement who could not hide either their happiness or their surprise at having voted for an African-American for president of the United States. In the '60s, they had withstood jailings, beatings and threats to their livelihoods, all because they wanted to be treated equally.

When Harris arrived to vote this time, her 80-year-old friend Mamie L. Nelson greeted her with a hug. "We marched, we sang and now it's happening," Nelson said. "It's really a feeling I cannot describe."

Boarding the campaign plane in
Indianapolis. October 23, 2008.

ABOVE: Rutha Mae Harris (right) seconds after learning of the election of Barack Obama as the 44th president of the United States. November 4, 2008.

BELOW: The Obamas voting in Chicago. November 4, 2008.

A thousand miles away, just before 6 a.m., Kimberly Ferguson was 12th in line on 125th Street in New York City. She was steps from Harlem's legendary Apollo Theater where African-American musicians such as Ella Fitzgerald, Aretha Franklin, James Brown and Stevie Wonder performed. "I got here early so I could make it to class," Ferguson said, shouldering a backpack of books with an orange peeking out of its side pocket.

One woman took a digital camera from her purse and photographed her neighbor as they waited in line. Instead of the smile-inducing "Cheese!" he said "Obama!" producing a wide grin and victory symbol.

Ferguson, who is a sophomore at Lehman College, appeared anxious. Today would be Ferguson's first-ever vote. And what lured her away from some extra shut-eye? She was voting, she said, for Barack Obama. Asked why, her solemn face melted to a grin.

"I want to be part of history," said Ferguson, who is majoring in black studies and minoring in education. All of her friends, she added, were also voting for Obama.

At 7:36 a.m. television cameras captured Barack and Michelle Obama as they arrived to vote, with their daughters, Malia, 10, and Sasha, 7, at Chicago's Beulah Shoesmith Elementary School. A few nights earlier, on Halloween, the candidate had briefly lost his cool when the cameras came too close while he walked Sasha, dressed as a corpse bride, to a neighborhood party. From this point onward, the Obamas and their young girls would be the focus of the kind of celebrity glare not seen since the early 1960s, when the Kennedy family was in the White House.

This was one reason Michelle Obama had taken so long to get comfortable with the idea of her husband

Supporters on Election Day, Athens, Ohio.
November 4, 2008.

running for president. She wanted her girls to have the kind of close family life that she and her brother Craig had enjoyed growing up on Chicago's South Side. There had been all too few family dinners since Feb. 10, 2007, when, standing in the front of Abraham Lincoln's Old State Capitol in Springfield, Ill., Barack Obama had declared his candidacy for president and recognized "there is a certain presumptuousness — a certain audacity — to this announcement."

Even Malia had found her father's fast rise bold. Visiting the U.S. Capitol shortly after his election to the Senate in 2004, she asked whether he would try to be president. Then a follow-up question so sensible it could only come from a first-grader, "Shouldn't you be vice president first?" The Clintons and other Democratic elders grumbled that Obama didn't have enough experience to run against a Republican veteran like John McCain. Senior leaders of the civil rights movement told him to wait his turn. Obama responded by quoting Dr. Martin Luther King Jr. on "the fierce urgency of now."

"THAT IS THE TRUE GENIUS OF AMERICA, A FAITH IN THE SIMPLE DREAMS OF ITS PEOPLE, THE INSISTENCE ON SMALL MIRACLES."

—BARACK OBAMA
JULY 24, 2004

DAMON WINTER/NYT

On election night, Barack and Michelle shared a steak dinner at home, then joined their circle of friends at a downtown hotel suite. There were the two Davids, Axelrod and Plouffe, the managers of strategies and the campaign respectively, as well as communications director Robert Gibbs. Valerie Jarrett, who had served as a mentor to both Barack and Michelle and, like them, was part of Chicago's black professional elite, embraced her friends. Children — the Obama girls and the grandchildren of Obama's running mate, Senator Joseph R. Biden Jr. of Delaware — bounced around the room.

Some of the key battleground states had already been called, but as the urban areas of Ohio began coming in, the candidate turned to Axelrod, who had been with him since Obama had been in the Illinois Senate.

Axelrod, a former political writer for the Chicago Sun-Times, had never worked for a winning presidential candidate.

According to Newsweek, Obama said, "It looks like we're going to win this thing, huh?"

DAVID GOLDMAN FOR NYT

ABOVE: At a rally in Minneapolis. February 2, 2008.

RIGHT: Post-election celebration in the streets of Harlem, New York City. November 5, 2008.

EVELYN HOCKSTEIN FOR NYT

JASON MILLER/AP

ABOVE: On Election Day, a performer guides a large Obama puppet in the streets of Cleveland, Ohio. November 4, 2008.

TOP RIGHT: Celebration at the Obama family homestead in western Kenya after the election results are announced. November 5, 2008.

"Yeah," nodded the red-eyed consultant.

From afar, the world watched. In Gaza, it seemed hardly possible that tens of millions of white Christians, voting freely, might select as their leader a black man, the son of a Muslim. There is a place on Earth — call it America — where such a thing could happen.

"We're going to the White House," sang the large crowd gathered in Kisumu, Kenya, where Obama's father was born and where much of his extended family still lives. Barack Obama Sr., haunted by alcoholism and poverty, had been killed in a 1982 car accident but some of the men and women who knew him would be staying up all night, swatting mosquitoes as they watched the election results on fuzzy-screened television sets.

In anticipation of a historic acceptance speech, crowds had been gathering in Chicago's Grant Park since daybreak.

And in Albany, Ga., Rutha Mae Harris was waiting and watching at Obama headquarters.

A SKINNY KID
WITH A FUNNY NAME

Barack Obama's parents met in Russian class at the University of Hawaii in 1960. His mother was white and had been born in Kansas. His father was a black man from Kenya.

Barack Sr. (his name meaning "blessed") was from the small village of Nyang'oma Kogelo near Lake Victoria, where as a boy he had helped tend his family's goats and attended school in a small shack. Now he was an economics student with a polished British accent. He captivated 18-year-old Stanley Ann Dunham (her father had wanted a boy and she was named for him, but she would later be known as Ann), and the two fell in love. They married in February 1961.

The Dunhams might have worried about the interracial match between Barack Sr. and their daughter, and Obama's family in Africa was none too thrilled over the marriage, either. All around the word in the '60s there was concern that blacks should not mix with whites.

A young Barack Obama takes a swing in Hawaii in the 1960s.

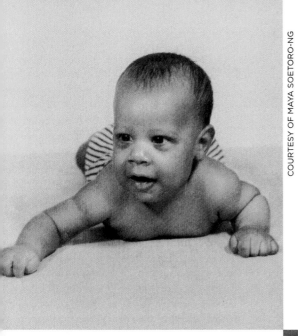

On Aug. 4, 1961, Barack Hussein Obama was born in Hawaii. But his father soon left his wife and child to attend Harvard in Cambridge, Mass., and returned to Africa after his graduation. He and Ann divorced in 1964 and young Barack would see his father only once again, when he was 10, during a monthlong visit in Hawaii. Barack Sr. had a different life, including wives and children back in Kenya. He died in a car accident in 1982.

ABOVE: Baby Barack.

RIGHT: Obama, 9, with his mother, Ann Dunham, his Indonesian stepfather, Lolo Soetoro, and baby sister Maya in Jakarta, Indonesia, in the 1970s.

BELOW: Playing in the sea in Hawaii in the 1960s.

After divorcing Barack Sr., Ann had remarried, to another foreign student at the University of Hawaii, Lolo Soetoro of Indonesia. The family moved to Jakarta, where Barack's half-sister, Maya, was born in 1970. He attended an Indonesian school, but to make sure her son kept up his English, Ann would wake him hours before school to study. When Barack complained about their 4 a.m. sessions, she replied, "This is no picnic for me either, Buster."

LEFT: Young Barack with his 5th grade class in 1972 at the Punahou Elementary School in Hawaii.

BELOW: "Barry O'Bomber" taking a jump shot over a defender at the Punahou School in Honolulu in 1979.

His stepfather bought Barack boxing gloves and taught him how to defend himself from bullies. But the marriage was strained and in 1971, Ann returned with her children to Hawaii to be near her parents. Through his boss, Barack's "Gramps" had arranged for Barack to enter fifth grade at Punahou, an elite prep school.

Barack's time at the school, where there were few other blacks, included learning the ways of the American upper class, which would prove helpful when he later attended Columbia University and Harvard Law School. Though he never felt that he fit in, Barack (who was nicknamed "Barry" by his father) found comfort on the basketball court, where he perfected a jump shot that earned him the name "Barry O'Bomber." When his mother returned to Indonesia to do field work for her Ph.D. in anthropology, Barack remained with his grandparents to finish his studies at Punahou.

In his memoir, "Dreams From My Father," Obama writes about his difficulties growing up. At school he heard a coach use racial slurs, and his own beloved grandmother "Toot" (an abbreviation for "tutu,"

ABOVE: Barack Obama's senior yearbook picture from the Punahou School, 1979.

RIGHT: The Illinois State Senator at a community meeting in his district.

BELOW: While a student at Columbia University.

which means "grandparent" in Hawaiian) would occasionally utter "racial or ethnic stereotypes that made me cringe," Obama recalled in his campaign speech on race. He had a pack of close friends and sometimes acted like a typical rebellious teenager. His mother and grandparents worried that he was slacking when it came to his studies, but Barack had begun a habit of disappearing behind his bedroom door to read powerful words written by black authors such as Richard Wright, James Baldwin and Malcolm X.

His search for identity continued at the small California liberal arts school Occidental College, and also at Columbia University in New York, where he transferred after two years.

After graduating from Columbia, Barack had difficulty getting hired as a community organizer, the job he wanted, and worked for a year at a business where he wore a suit. He could have started down a path toward money and status, but he wanted to make a difference in people's lives.

In 1985, Gerald Kellman, a community organizer in Chicago's tough South Side, interviewed Barack and was surprised that he "challenged me on whether

we would teach him anything," Kellman recalled. "He wanted to know things like 'How are you going to train me?' and 'What am I going to learn?'" With a $10,000 salary and $2,000 to buy a used car, Obama began a three-year stint as a grassroots organizer in Chicago's housing projects and churches.

As he wrote in his first book, Obama felt that the job was "the best education I ever had, better than anything I got at Harvard Law School." He learned to listen to people's concerns about their community and helped them improve their lives. Through his efforts, he helped clean up a housing project for the poor.

> "… WHETHER PEOPLE WERE FRIENDLY, INDIFFERENT, OR OCCASIONALLY HOSTILE, I TRIED MY BEST TO KEEP MY MOUTH SHUT AND HEAR WHAT THEY HAD TO SAY."
>
> —BARACK OBAMA
> "THE AUDACITY OF HOPE"

THE WOMAN WHO SHAPED HIM

Despite his father's large presence in "Dreams From My Father," Barack Obama's free-spirited mother, Stanley Ann Dunham Soetoro, was the parent who most shaped him. "I know that she was the kindest, most generous spirit I have ever known, and that what is best in me I owe to her," he wrote.

His half-sister, Maya Soetoro-Ng, has said that their mother's most difficult decision was to leave her son to finish high school in Hawaii while she pursued her studies in Indonesia. "She wanted him to be with her," Soetoro-Ng recalled. But she also recognized that while it was painful to be separated, "it was perhaps the best thing for him."

When Obama was in high school, his mother confronted him about his seeming lack of ambition, Obama wrote. He could get into any college in the country, she told him, with just a little effort. ("Remember what that's like? Effort?") He says he looked at her, so certain and sure of his destiny: "I suddenly felt like puncturing that certainty of hers, letting her know that her experiment with me had failed."

Of course, the experiment was hardly a failure. "There were certainly times in his life in those four years when he could have used her presence on a more daily basis," said Soetoro-Ng, who became an anthropologist like her mother. "But I think he did all right for himself."

Obama now speaks of his mother with a mix of love and regret. He has said his biggest mistake was not being at her bedside when she died in 1995. And when The Associated Press asked the candidates about "prized keepsakes" — others mentioned signed baseballs or a pocket watch — Obama said his was a photograph of the cliffs of the South Shore of Oahu in Hawaii where his mother's ashes were scattered.

Mother and son in the 1970s.

Barack Obama throws a lei at the spot where he once scattered his mother's ashes, Honolulu. August 14, 2008.

AN ABSENT FATHER

Ten-year-old Barack Obama was filled with dread in 1971 when he was reunited with his father for the one and only time, in Honolulu, Hawaii, during the Christmas season. A visit had been arranged for his Kenyan father to speak to Barack's class at Punahou. "I couldn't imagine worse news," he wrote in "Dreams From My Father." "I spent that night and all of the next day trying to suppress thoughts of the inevitable: the faces of my classmates when they heard about mud huts . . . the painful jokes afterward."

Barack was still the new kid at Punahou. The classroom visit, as it turned out, went well enough (one student told Barack he thought his father was "cool") but the monthlong family reunion was sometimes strained. His father, who needed a cane to walk, was frailer than his son anticipated. He was also strict. When he thought Barack was ignoring his studies and watching too much television, a family fight, including his mother and grandparents, erupted

over whether Barack would be allowed to watch the rest of "How the Grinch Stole Christmas."

There were pleasant times, too, including a visit to a jazz club and the Christmas gift of an orange basketball.

During his visit with his ex-wife and son, Barack Sr. suggested the idea of getting the family, including Maya, back together. But even though Ann had broken up with her second husband, she refused him.

According to Barack, before his departure, his father had one last lesson for him. "Come, Barry, you will learn from the master," he said, as he retrieved two dusty records from his suitcase and put them on the stereo. "Suddenly his slender body was swaying back and forth, the lush sound was rising." And the son began to dance.

Barack Obama's father's short life ended in a car accident in Nairobi at age 46 in 1982.

LEFT: Barack Sr. and his 10-year-old son.

A GRANDMOTHER'S LOVE

For the last 21 months, she had followed his presidential campaign like a spectator on a faraway balcony.

She underwent eye surgery to better see him on television. In one of their frequent telephone conversations she told him that it might not hurt if he smiled a bit more.

And, just 11 days before the election, Barack Obama suspended his campaign to spend a day in Honolulu saying good-bye.

At the Punahou Circle Apartments, a place of Obama's own childhood, Madelyn Dunham, his grandmother, lay ill, suffering from cancer and other ailments. When she was released from the hospital after surgery to repair a broken hip, the doctors told him that she didn't have much time left.

He announced to his campaign advisers that he had to make the trip to say good-bye to his grandmother no matter what. He was absent when his mother died in 1995, a mistake he said he did not intend to repeat with her mother. She lay in the same apartment where Obama lived from the age of 10, now filled with flowers and good wishes from strangers who wrote that they had come to know her from his first book, "Dreams From My Father." Also present was his sister, Maya.

"One of the things I wanted to make sure of is that I had a chance to sit down with her and talk to her," Obama said on the ABC News television program "Good Morning America." "She's still alert and she's still got all her faculties, and I want to make sure that — that I don't miss that opportunity right now."

As Obama flew west across six time zones on his way to see her, he remained alone in the front of his campaign plane. It was a very different mood from that during a flight nine months earlier, when he made a trip to Kansas for his first visit to the town of El Dorado, where his maternal grandparents had originally lived.

A smile washed over his face on that late January day as he spoke about the woman he called Toot.

"She can't travel," he told reporters then. "She has a bad back. She has pretty severe osteoporosis. But she's glued to CNN."

Back then, when he was in the opening stages of his Democratic primary fight, he spoke wistfully about his grandparents, whose all-American biography had become critical to establishing his own story. He told of how his grandfather, Stanley, who died in 1992, had fought in World War II while his grandmother worked on war planes at a plant in Wichita, Kan.

"My grandparents held on to a simple dream: that they would raise my mother in a land of boundless dreams," Obama said. "I am standing here today because that dream was realized."

In August, as he prepared to accept the Democratic nomination, Obama delivered a long-distance message to Toot in a televised speech.

"Thank you to my grandmother, who helped raise me and is sitting in Hawaii somewhere right now because she can't travel, but who poured everything she had into me and who helped me become the man I am today," Obama said. "Tonight is for her."

Sadly, Madelyn Dunham, 86, did not live to see him elected.

"She has gone home," Obama announced at a late campaign stop in North Carolina the day before the election. His voice was tinged with emotion. "She died peacefully in her sleep with my sister at her side, so there's great joy instead of tears."

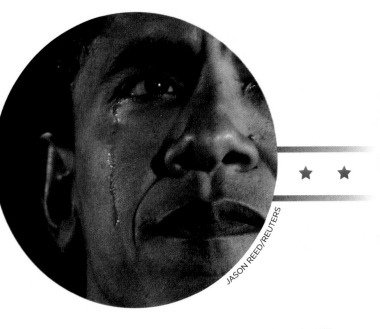

LEFT: The high school graduate with his grandmother in 1979.

RIGHT: The candidate weeps while speaking of his grandmother during a rally in Charlotte, N.C. She had died earlier, just a day short of his election. November 3, 2008.

JASON REED/REUTERS

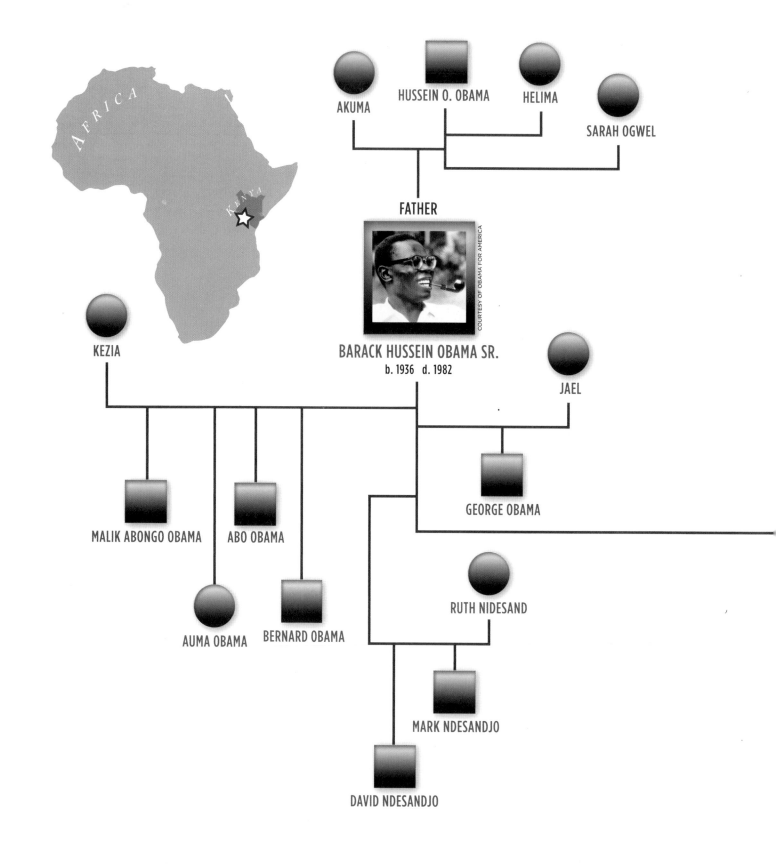

AKUMA HUSSEIN O. OBAMA HELIMA SARAH OGWEL

FATHER

COURTESY OF OBAMA FOR AMERICA

BARACK HUSSEIN OBAMA SR.
b. 1936   d. 1982

KEZIA

JAEL

MALIK ABONGO OBAMA   ABO OBAMA

GEORGE OBAMA

AUMA OBAMA   BERNARD OBAMA

RUTH NIDESAND

MARK NDESANDJO

DAVID NDESANDJO

FAMILY TREE

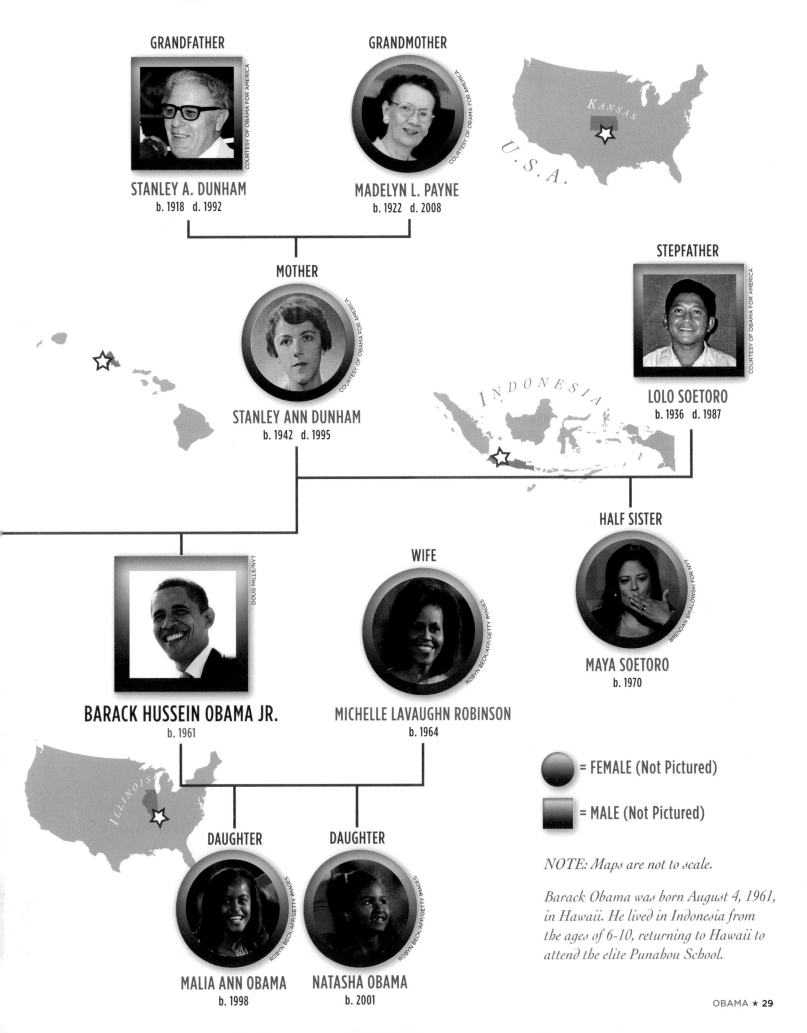

GRANDFATHER

STANLEY A. DUNHAM
b. 1918   d. 1992

GRANDMOTHER

MADELYN L. PAYNE
b. 1922   d. 2008

KANSAS

U.S.A.

MOTHER

STANLEY ANN DUNHAM
b. 1942   d. 1995

STEPFATHER

LOLO SOETORO
b. 1936   d. 1987

INDONESIA

HALF SISTER

MAYA SOETORO
b. 1970

WIFE

MICHELLE LAVAUGHN ROBINSON
b. 1964

BARACK HUSSEIN OBAMA JR.
b. 1961

ILLINOIS

DAUGHTER

MALIA ANN OBAMA
b. 1998

DAUGHTER

NATASHA OBAMA
b. 2001

= FEMALE (Not Pictured)

= MALE (Not Pictured)

NOTE: Maps are not to scale.

Barack Obama was born August 4, 1961, in Hawaii. He lived in Indonesia from the ages of 6-10, returning to Hawaii to attend the elite Punahou School.

THE PATH
OF A POLITICIAN

Before attending Harvard Law School, Barack Obama traveled to Kenya for the first time. There he met his father's family: his African half-brothers and half-sisters and his step-grandmother, Sarah, who helped raise his father in the same way his own grandmother, Toot, looked after Barack. His father was well known, and Barack suddenly understood what it meant to belong; everyone seemed to know him, too.

He returned to the United States to begin law school. At 27, he was older than most of the other first-year students at Harvard and at the end of the year he won a position as one of about 80 editors of the law review publication, which was the most influential in the country. That summer, while working in a Chicago law firm he met and fell in love with another young Harvard Law grad, Michelle Robinson. They continued a long-distance relationship.

Harvard Law School student Barack Obama.

The next year, in February 1990, he won the law review's presidency. Obama sometimes joked that the presidency of the Harvard Law Review was the second-hardest election in the country to win — next to president of the United States, that is. He was the first black elected in its 104-year history.

"The fact that I've been elected shows a lot of progress," he told New York Times correspondent Fox Butterfield. "But it's important that stories like mine aren't used to say that everything is O.K. for blacks. You have to remember that for every one of me, there are hundreds or thousands of black students with at least equal talent who don't get a chance," he said, alluding to poverty or growing up in a drug environment.

After graduating Harvard he returned to Chicago, where he worked on a voter registration drive and registered nearly 150,000 new voters, joined a small law firm specializing in civil rights cases and taught

TOP LEFT: The Harvard Law Review Board of Editors for the 1990-1991 academic year. Obama is at center, holding the staff.

ABOVE: After law school, Obama returned to Chicago, where he ran a voter registration drive in 1992.

RIGHT: Teaching at the University of Chicago Law School.

> **"HOPE IS THAT THING INSIDE US THAT INSISTS, DESPITE ALL EVIDENCE TO THE CONTRARY, THAT SOMETHING BETTER AWAITS US IF WE HAVE THE COURAGE TO REACH FOR IT, AND TO WORK FOR IT, AND TO FIGHT FOR IT."**
>
> **—BARACK OBAMA**
> JANUARY 3, 2008

at the University of Chicago Law School. In 1992, he and Michelle were married.

In 1995, Obama's first book, "Dreams From My Father," was published. In it, he describes his struggle to understand his place in the world. Growing up black with a white mother and grandparents was sometimes difficult, but he gradually learned to appreciate both sides of his heritage.

MICHELLE OBAMA

Though she attended the prestigious Princeton University and Harvard Law School, Michelle Obama was still a tough girl from the South Side of Chicago. Before her husband gave the 2004 keynote speech at the Democratic convention she told him, "Just don't screw it up, buddy." Before she would give her blessing for the presidential run, she made him promise to give up smoking, a promise he's not kept completely yet.

More than many other candidates, Barack Obama openly talked about the strains the campaign put on his family. At one of the final debates, his voice cracked when he talked about leaving his daughters to fly back to Washington for a vote. In 2006, at a Washington party for his book "The Audacity of Hope," he became tearful while recognizing the sacrifices his family had made for his career. When he couldn't continue, Michelle came up, threw her arms around him and kissed his cheeks.

Michelle grew up in a house with "two bedrooms, if you want to be generous," she said. Her father, Fraser Robinson, a city pump operator, suffered from multiple sclerosis and died in 1991. The Robinsons sent both Michelle and her brother Craig to Princeton. Michelle was one of 94 black freshmen in a class of over 1,100. She roomed with a white student whose mother pleaded with Princeton to give her daughter a white roommate instead. Princeton was followed by Harvard Law, then the Chicago firm Sidley & Austin, where Barack Obama arrived as a summer associate in 1989.

He romanced her with ice cream and invitations to hear him speak at community

FROM TOP: Michelle Obama in grade school; her Princeton University graduation picture, 1985; Barack and Michelle's wedding day, October 18, 1992; and giving her husband a fist bump before he claims the Democratic nomination on June 3, 2008.

groups. They were married Oct. 18, 1992, in Chicago's Trinity United Church of Christ with the Rev. Jeremiah A. Wright Jr. officiating.

She managed to be the primary bread-winner and, after the girls were born, mother. Known for her 4:30 a.m. workout sessions and meals prepared Rachael Ray style, in less than 30 minutes, her friends came up with still another nickname, "The Taskmaster."

"I come here as a wife who loves my husband and believes he will be an extraordinary president," she said in her speech at the 2008 Democratic Convention. "I come here as a mom whose girls are the heart of my heart and the center of my world. They're the first thing I think about when I wake up in the morning and the last thing I think about when I go to bed at night. Their future and all our children's future is my stake in this election."

CHICAGO POLITICS

Obama had politics on his mind as he moved to Hyde Park. A tight-knit community that runs through Chicago's South Side, Hyde Park has a diverse population in what is otherwise one of the nation's most segregated cities, with the University of Chicago at its center.

In 1995, Obama, a Democrat, kicked off his candidacy for the Illinois State Senate at the same Hyde Park hotel where Harold Washington, the city's first black mayor, had announced his candidacy. He won the seat and learned to navigate the heavily Democratic political scene.

In 2002, as Washington prepared to go to war in Iraq, Obama made an antiwar speech, something unusual for a state legislator. He called the war in Iraq "dumb," while carefully pointing out that he was not opposed to all wars. His early stand against the war gave him a defining issue when he later ran for president.

Unexpectedly, a seat in the U.S. Senate opened up in 2004 and Obama decided to run. That same year, he was selected to give the keynote speech — an important address that is used to set the tone and summarize the overall message — at the 2004 Democratic convention. He set the convention on fire with his youthful energy and powerful words. He later won the election in Chicago with 70 percent of the popular vote and became only the third black elected to the United States Senate since the end of the Civil War.

Each state elects two senators to represent them in Washington, D.C., and Obama was 99th in seniority (out of 100 senators, he was one of the newest members). At committee hearings he had to wait to speak until the end.

He missed his family, especially daughters Malia and Sasha. He and Michelle had decided not to move the family, so Obama

RICHARD PERRY/NYT

M. SPENCER GREEN/AP

LEFT: Obama at a preschool in his district.

ABOVE AND RIGHT: Giving the keynote speech at the 2004 Democratic National Convention in Boston and celebrating his new Senate post with his family at a post-election party in Chicago on November 2, 2004.

commuted between Washington and Chicago. He was much younger than most of his Senate colleagues and most nights he opted to go to the gym alone.

In the fall of 2006, his second book, "The Audacity of Hope," was published. It was an examination of his political views as well as his belief that each one of us has the ability to make a difference in the world. Oprah Winfrey chose it for her book club and it quickly became a bestseller. And Obama began considering a run for the presidency.

THE PRIMARY
RACE

Making the decision to run for president wasn't easy for Barack Obama. His wife, Michelle, worried about his safety and their family life. They both knew that in order to win, Obama wouldn't be able to spend much time with his daughters. He would have to spend nearly two years campaigning across the country, introducing himself and learning about voters' concerns. Over a Christmas vacation in Hawaii in 2006, they visited his grandmother, Toot, and took long walks to discuss the future. Finally, a decision had to be made.

After hearing the pros and cons from their closest political advisers and trusted friends, Michelle turned to her husband.

The candidate runs to the stage during a rally at Knology Park, Dunedin, Fla. September 24, 2008.

WHAT IS A PRIMARY?

A primary is a preliminary election in which registered voters of a political party choose a candidate for a later, general election.

★

★

★

WHAT IS A CAUCUS?
A caucus is a meeting of members of a political party in which a candidate for the general election is chosen.

"You need to ask yourself, Why do you want to do this? What are you hoping to accomplish, Barack?"

He sat quietly for a moment and then responded: "This I know: When I raise my hand and take that oath of office, I think the world will look at us differently. And millions of kids across this country will look at themselves differently."

America, he believed, was ready for change.

Obama made his announcement to run for president on Feb. 10, 2007. He stood before the Old State Capitol in Springfield, Ill., where Abraham Lincoln began his political career, and used Lincoln's famous words, "a house divided against itself cannot stand."

"The time for that politics is over," he said. "It's time to turn the page. . . . Each and every time, a new generation has risen up and done what's needed to be done. Today we are called once more, and it is time for our generation to answer that call."

> "THE TIME HAS COME FOR A PRESIDENT WHO WILL BE HONEST ABOUT THE CHOICES AND THE CHALLENGES WE FACE; WHO WILL LISTEN TO YOU AND LEARN FROM YOU EVEN WHEN WE DISAGREE; WHO WON'T JUST TELL YOU WHAT YOU WANT TO HEAR, BUT WHAT YOU NEED TO KNOW."
> —BARACK OBAMA
> JANUARY 3, 2008

JOSH HANER/NYT

PHOTOS: RUTH FREMSON/NYT

LEFT: *Barack Obama's formal announcement of his run for the presidency, Springfield, Ill. February 10, 2007.*

★ ★ ★ ★ ★

WHAT IS A DELEGATE?

A delegate is a state representative at a political party's national convention, where the nominee for president must win the majority of the delegates' votes. Delegates are pledged to support the candidate chosen in their state's primary election.

The Democratic Party also has "superdelegates" who are not bound by state elections and are thus free to support a candidate regardless of voter preference. Superdelegates include elected officials such as members of Congress and governors. The Republican Party has no superdelegates.

FAR LEFT: *An early Democratic presidential debate in Charleston, S.C. From left, Senator Christopher Dodd of Connecticut, former Senator John Edwards of North Carolina, Senator Hillary Rodham Clinton of New York, Senator Barack Obama of Illinois, Governor Bill Richardson of New Mexico, Senator Joseph R. Biden Jr. of Delaware and Representative Dennis Kucinich of Ohio. July 23, 2007.*

One of Obama's staff members later asked him how he had prevented his teeth from chattering in the cold. It turned out that a heater had been placed at his feet, so that the audience couldn't see.

For Obama, former first lady and current New York Senator Hillary Rodham Clinton was his main opponent for the Democratic nomination. Obama hoped to win by a large margin in the first race, in Iowa in early January. His plan called for using the Internet to create enthusiasm, raise record sums of money and build an organization of volunteers across the state. The campaign's main theme was change.

Hillary Clinton, along with several other early contenders during the primary election, said that Obama didn't have enough political experience. But it turned out that Iowa Democrats were on Obama's side, and Hillary had a disappointing third-place finish, after Sen. John Edwards of North Carolina. Next: New Hampshire, where Obama came in second behind Clinton.

"I guess this is going to go on for awhile," Obama said when aides delivered the disappointing results.

He won South Carolina with a huge margin among black voters and the endorsements of Sen. Edward M. Kennedy and his niece, Caroline, who had never before endorsed a political candidate outside her family.

The two candidates continued to debate, although they shared the same opinion on most major issues. Many voters were impressed by Clinton's résumé as former first lady and senator, but Obama built an exciting campaign around the theme of change. It was a historic race because regardless of which candidate would eventually secure the Democratic nomination, it would be an American first — either the first female or the first African-American presidential candidate from a major political party.

ABOVE: Shadrick Johnson, 6, was dressed in his Sunday best as he waited to see Senator Obama in Columbia, S.C. January 20, 2008.

BELOW: Supporters engulf the Democratic hopeful in St. Paul. June 3, 2008.

"YEARS FROM NOW, YOU'LL LOOK BACK AND YOU'LL SAY THAT THIS WAS THE MOMENT—THIS WAS THE PLACE— WHERE AMERICA REMEMBERED WHAT IT MEANS TO HOPE."

—BARACK OBAMA
JANUARY 3, 2008

For luck, every day Obama played basketball with Reggie Love, 26, his personal assistant. At 6-foot-5, Love, who played football and basketball at Duke University, was about three inches taller than the tall candidate, and physically fitter.

"There's no doubt that Reggie is cooler than I am," Obama said of his sidekick. "I am living vicariously through Reggie."

Obama did make mistakes. He was caught by a Web site blogger describing some white, working-class voters as "bitter." And his pastor, Rev. Jeremiah Wright's more outrageous sermons almost derailed his candidacy. (See p. 44.)

On June 3, the final day of the long primary season, he won just enough votes to become the Democratic nominee. Almost immediately, people began wondering if he would choose Hillary Clinton as his running mate.

DOUG MILLS/NYT

ABOVE: Reggie Love and the candidate after a pickup basketball game in Chicago on primary day. May 20, 2008.

RIGHT: Senators Obama and Clinton campaigning together for the first time in the town of Unity, N.H. June 27, 2008.

TYLER HICKS/NYT

DOUG MILLS/NYT

A CONTROVERSIAL FATHER FIGURE

If his father was a missing presence in Barack Obama's life, another older black man emerged to fill the vacuum: the Rev. Jeremiah A. Wright Jr. He married the Obamas in 1992, baptized their daughters and blessed their home.

The two met in the 1980s, while Obama was working as a community organizer in Chicago. Wright had built Trinity United Church of Christ into a diverse, 6,000-member congregation.

Prior to meeting Wright, Obama's religious education had been focused more on the bits and pieces of different religions that appealed to his mother. His grandparents were non-practicing Baptists and Methodists. In Indonesia, he had attended a Catholic school and a public school and while Punahou, the school he attended in Hawaii, had been founded by Christian missionaries, it did not stress formal religion.

Joining Wright's church helped Obama embrace not only the African-American community but also Africa. He had known little about the beliefs of his Kenyan father; Wright traveled to Africa often and incorporated African rituals into worship.

Wright saw the Bible as the story of the struggles of African-Americans. People flocked to hear his blunt, charismatic preaching. But Wright's message was often radical.

Just as Barack Obama was hoping to beat Hillary Clinton in a set of spring primaries, Wright came roaring into the headlines. In March, video of Wright making negative, divisive statements about America appeared on YouTube. Many people were offended by these remarks and wondered how Obama could choose such a man as his pastor and friend.

The minister's defenders tried to explain that the statements were taken out of context, but the controversy continued to grow.

Relations between Obama and Wright had been strained since Obama announced that he was running for president. Wright was originally supposed to perform an invocation — the blessing or the opening prayer — at the announcement, but Obama's campaign directors feared that Wright would attract controversy and Obama canceled it at the last minute. This hurt the pastor deeply.

Despite Obama's attempt to distance himself from Wright's most radical sermons, the pastor continued to make headlines with his views, and polls indicated that the relationship between the two men was harming Obama's candidacy.

Obama decided to give a speech on race in Philadelphia. He wrote every word himself rather than use a speechwriter to help him. The speech was a powerful call for the country to rise above the use of race as a way to divide Americans.

"We have a choice in this country," he said. "We can accept a politics that breeds division and conflict and cynicism."

Or, he said, Americans could move in a different direction. "At this moment, in this election, we can come together and say, 'Not this time.' This time, we want to talk about the crumbling schools that are stealing the future of black children and white children and Asian children and Hispanic children and Native-American children. . . ."

About Wright, Obama said, "As imperfect as he may be, he has been like family to me," adding: "Not once in my conversations with him have I heard him talk about any ethnic group in derogatory terms."

That might have ended the story, but Wright continued to make comments that many people found offensive. Finally, Obama cut all ties with the pastor and announced that he and his family were leaving Trinity Church.

★ ★

Rev. Jeremiah Wright Jr. at the National Press Club in Washington, D.C. April 28, 2008.

THE GENERAL
ELECTION

While Barack Obama projected an image of youth and change, John McCain, the Republican nominee, who turned 72 during the campaign, was running on his image of experience. A former prisoner of war in Vietnam, the Arizona senator was admired for his no-nonsense approach to politics and independent stands on issues.

He had wrapped up his party's nomination in early March, which should have given him plenty of time to campaign while Obama and Hillary Rodham Clinton fought in the Democratic primaries. But because he was running as a Republican, McCain was connected to an unpopular president, George W. Bush. He was also a fervent supporter of the war in Iraq, insisting the United States was winning the conflict. Obama disagreed and had promised to end the war.

Republican presidential candidate Sen. John McCain and Democratic presidential candidate Sen. Barack Obama take part in the presidential debate at Belmont University in Nashville, Tenn. October 7, 2008.

TOP LEFT: France's President Nicolas Sarkozy welcomes the candidate to the Élysée Palace in Paris. July 25, 2008.

BELOW LEFT: Senator Obama with his running mate, Senator Joseph R. Biden Jr. of Delaware, Springfield, Ill. August 23, 2008.

RIGHT: Arriving to deliver a speech at the Victory Column in Tiergarten Park in Berlin. July 24, 2008.

But national security was not the main issue in this election. By the fall, the country was in a full-out financial crisis, requiring an emergency federal bailout of the country's leading financial institutions to make sure that people's savings accounts were protected. The government also stepped in to prevent massive job losses. Many Americans blamed the Republican administration for the economy's downturn. Since McCain was a Republican, this did not bode well for him.

The only strategy that seemed to make a win possible under such circumstances was to focus on negative statements about Obama, but McCain saw himself as a man of honor and resisted. In late July, Obama toured the Middle East and Europe on a trip intended to make him appear presidential. After Obama appeared before a huge crowd at the Brandenburg Gate in Berlin, however, the McCain team began airing an attack ad portraying him as "the biggest celebrity in the world," alternating his Berlin speech with pictures of Britney Spears and Paris Hilton. They thought this would make Obama seem silly and concerned only with fame.

The Obama campaign, buoyed by strong fund-raising, immediately aired forceful responses to the attacks. His campaign eventually raised $750 million, hundreds of millions more than McCain.

In a tactic designed to appeal to younger voters and build online excitement, Obama had promised his supporters that he would announce his vice-presidential selection in a mass e-mail. The pick was Senator Joseph R. Biden Jr. of Delaware. Biden's experience in foreign affairs helped to weaken McCain's claims that Obama didn't have a strong enough background in national security.

ABOVE: The Biden announcement was first delivered via text message early Saturday morning. August 23, 2008.

BELOW: The line for the entrance to Invesco Field at Mile High Stadium, where Barack Obama was to make his acceptance speech at the Democratic National Convention, Denver, Colo. August 28, 2008.

During the Democratic convention in Denver, Colo., where Obama's nomination became official, former president Bill Clinton gave Obama a gracious endorsement. Hillary Clinton also gave a warm speech, unifying the Democratic Party that had seemed so badly fractured in the primaries.

For the final night of the convention, the campaign had decided to move everyone to Invesco Field at Mile

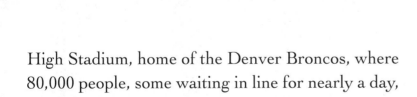

ABOVE: Michelle Obama addresses the Democratic National Convention in Denver, Colo. August 25, 2008.

LEFT: Senator Barack Obama and his running mate, Joe Biden, with their wives, Michelle and Jill, at the convention. August 28, 2008.

BELOW: Senator Hillary Clinton delivered her address on the second day of the convention. August 26, 2008.

OPPOSITE PAGE: Accepting his party's nomination for president at Invesco Field at Mile High Stadium. August 28, 2008.

High Stadium, home of the Denver Broncos, where 80,000 people, some waiting in line for nearly a day, celebrated the new Democratic ticket.

"With profound gratitude and great humility, I accept your nomination for the presidency of the United States," Obama began. The speech was being delivered on the 45th anniversary of Dr. Martin Luther King Jr.'s "I Have a Dream" speech.

> "I'VE GOT NEWS FOR YOU, JOHN MCCAIN. WE ALL PUT OUR COUNTRY FIRST."
>
> **—BARACK OBAMA**
> AUGUST 28, 2008

ABOVE: Senator John McCain and his running mate, Alaska Governor Sarah Palin.

The next day, John McCain announced his choice for vice president: a young female governor, Sarah Palin of Alaska. His selection excited many Republicans. But some worried the choice undermined McCain's major campaign theme, experience. Palin wasn't very experienced in politics: she had been governor only a few years, and before that was the mayor of a tiny town, Wasilla. Most people had never seen her before the Republican National Convention in St. Paul, Minn.

After rejoicing over her strong convention acceptance speech, in which she relentlessly attacked and mocked Obama, the McCain campaign kept her from the national media. Then, after helping her prepare for weeks, interviews with the network anchors were scheduled. Her performance during an interview with Katie Couric, in which she stumbled repeatedly over relatively simple questions, became popular on YouTube and was portrayed mockingly on "Saturday Night Live."

Once the election shifted to Democrats versus Republicans, the dynamics changed. Unlike the

LIVE FROM NEW YORK!

DAMON WINTER/NYT

DANA EDELSON/NBC

With her signature black glasses, Sarah Palin, the Republican nominee for vice president, looked a lot like Tina Fey, the creator of NBC's "30 Rock" and former "Saturday Night Live" writer and star. Soon Fey was back on "SNL" doing an impersonation of Palin (above right) that helped the show score its highest ratings in years.

Fey, along with another "SNL" star, Amy Poehler, who played the CBS anchor Katie Couric (in a previous skit, Poehler had played Hillary Rodham Clinton), parodied Palin's performance during the interview. Many people felt that Palin was unprepared for the vice presidency, and the skits on "SNL" exaggerated her inexperience. When it came to a question about spreading democracy in other countries, Fey, rather than answer the question, acted as if she was on a game show and said, "Katie, I'd like to use one of my lifelines," adding later, "I want to phone a friend." The joke implied that Sarah Palin had no idea how to respond and needed assistance to answer the question.

Fey made her final appearance as Palin on "SNL" alongside the real John McCain. They appeared with his wife, Cindy McCain, in a skit where the money-strapped McCain-Palin ticket went on the QVC shopping network to "sell stuff" to raise money for the campaign. Many people saw it as the McCain-Palin team's attempt to join in on the jokes and show that they weren't bothered by them.

POOL PHOTO BY GARY HERSHORN

★ ★ ★ **ISSUES: OBAMA** ★ ★ ★

IRAQ WAR: Favors troop withdrawal and focusing resources on Afghanistan

TAXES: Tax the rich; go easy on the middle and lower classes

HEALTH CARE: Health insurance required for children; aims for universal coverage

CLIMATE ISSUES: Says U.S. must lead global efforts to reduce emissions; would institute cap-and-trade system, requiring companies to bid for the right to emit greenhouse gases

ENERGY: Opposes drilling in the Arctic; says oil companies should exploit existing leases before new areas are opened to drilling

ABORTION: Proponent of abortion rights

GAY MARRIAGE AND ADOPTION: Opposes gay marriage but also opposes a federal constitutional amendment to ban it, as well as a California effort to ban it; supports civil unions and supports gay adoptions

GUN CONTROL: Supports some restrictions on gun ownership

DEATH PENALTY: Supports the death penalty for certain crimes

primaries, where Obama and Clinton had agreed on more issues than not, Obama and McCain had extremely different views.

Their major differences were over the war in Iraq. McCain still spoke of "victory" and didn't want to set dates for removing American troops. Obama was against the war from the start and wanted to withdraw American forces. He blamed President Bush for taking his focus off defeating Al Qaeda and becoming distracted by Iraq.

They differed over the role of government in people's lives. McCain was an economic conservative who railed against wasteful government spending. In his convention speech in Denver, Obama said: "Government cannot solve all our problems, but what it should do is that which we cannot do for ourselves: protect us from harm and provide every child a decent education; keep our water clean and our toys safe; invest in new schools and new roads and new science and technology."

They also differed on the kinds of justices they would appoint to the Supreme Court. Obama favored abortion rights, while McCain opposed them.

Earlier in his career, McCain had offered the first realistic bill to control America's emissions of greenhouse gases. In this campaign, McCain abandoned his former positions on climate change and immigration reform.

Obama presented himself as an environmental protector who would strictly control the emissions of greenhouse gases. He promised to create thousands of new "green collar" jobs that would revolve around clean-air technology.

Right before the candidates' first debate, the economy tanked. Lehman Brothers, a major investment bank, collapsed, an indicator of the coming financial crisis and a reminder that the presidential campaign was turning into a contest on which candidate could best address the nation's economic concerns.

Speaking at an almost empty convention center in Jacksonville, Fla., on Sept. 15, McCain was trying to show concern while also remaining optimistic that things would improve.

"The fundamentals of our economy are strong," he said. Some believe that these words cost him the election.

By nightfall, the Obama campaign had produced an advertisement that included video of McCain making the statement, a vision that would shadow him for the rest of the campaign. If the economy was strong, many people wondered, why does everything from gas to milk cost so much money? And why are so many people not able to afford the mortgage payments on their homes?

Obama's calm performance in their first debate made him appear presidential. McCain did not look at Obama once during the 90-minute debate, despite rules that encouraged them to speak directly to each other.

The second and third debates were really no better for McCain. In various polls, Obama was deemed the winner of all three debates. Well-prepared and commanding, if not exciting, he had come across as a plausible president.

Then, former Secretary of State Colin L. Powell endorsed Obama in late October. He believed strongly that Obama was the better candidate. This came as a surprise to many since Powell was a member of the Republican Party and had served in three Republican administrations.

With plenty of money still flowing into the campaign during the final month, Obama bought a half-hour of national television time for an infomercial. A smashing ratings success, the commercial proved to be more popular than even the final game of the World Series — or last season's finale of "American Idol."

POOL PHOTO BY GARY HERSHORN

★ ★ **ISSUES: MCCAIN** ★ ★

IRAQ WAR: Favors pursuing victory in Iraq; against troop withdrawal

TAXES: Cut everyone's taxes; permanently implement Bush's tax cuts

HEALTH CARE: Opposes universal coverage; wants to give individuals right to choose health care via tax credits

CLIMATE ISSUES: Says U.S. should work toward a global effort that would include developing countries

ENERGY: Opposes drilling in the Arctic; now supports expanded drilling offshore

ABORTION: Anti-abortion

GAY MARRIAGE AND ADOPTION: Opposes gay marriage but also opposes a constitutional amendment to ban it; supports the California effort to ban gay marriage; has been ambiguous about civil unions

GUN CONTROL: Opposes gun control

DEATH PENALTY: Supports expanding the federal death penalty

THE SCARS OF YESTERDAY

The Rev. Martin Luther King Jr. delivered his famous "I Have a Dream" speech for racial equality at the March on Washington, which took place on Aug. 28, 1963, in front of hundreds of thousands of people at the Lincoln Memorial in Washington, D.C. The March is seen as one of the most important events in the civil rights movement.

At least five veterans of that March on Washington traveled to the Democratic National Convention in Denver in August 2008. One of them, Representative John Lewis of Georgia, is the last man alive of the 10 who spoke that day at the Lincoln Memorial. A son of sharecroppers, Lewis was once almost beaten to death by police officers in Selma, Ala., when he marched across a bridge in peaceful protest with civil rights activists.

Barack Obama was only a toddler when Lewis was part of the civil rights movement. He doesn't remember that many restaurants and hotels in the South were segregated and didn't allow black customers. Even water fountains sometimes read, "For Whites Only." It wasn't until the Civil Rights Act of 1964 that racial segregation in schools, public places and employment was made illegal.

John Lewis remembers — and Obama's nomination was very important to him.

"We've had disappointments since then, but if someone told me I would be here," Lewis said, shaking his head. "When people say nothing has changed, I feel like saying, 'Come walk in my shoes.'"

Dezie Woods-Jones had also been in Washington to hear King speak about his dream. Now in her 60s, she admitted, "About 10 years ago I thought: I won't see this. This is something for my grandchildren."

She paused, her eyes now red with tears.

"What to say except, 'Oh, hallelujah!'" she said. "We have a lot of work, a lot, but we are so much closer than I expected."

ERIK S. LESSER FOR NYT

ABOVE: Senator Obama joins Representative John Lewis at a church in Selma, Ala. March 4, 2008.

RIGHT: A voter casts his ballot in the Democratic primary at Martin Luther King Jr. Park in Columbia, S.C. January 26, 2008.

DAMON WINTER/NYT

5

VICTORY

When Senator Barack Obama stepped from his plane on the final ride of his presidential candidacy, he did something he had not done before while on the campaign trail: He saluted.

The salute was a gesture of thanks to a group of his campaign workers, who had gathered at Midway Airport in Chicago to watch him arrive from his last trip, a short hop from nearby Indiana. It was a moment many would remember as the foreshadowing of events to come, as the salute made Obama look very much like a president.

In the final hours of a 22-month campaign, he quickly moved on to a superstitious election day tradition: basketball. He had skipped his afternoon game twice during the primaries on the day votes were cast. And both times he lost.

So at 2:45 p.m. Obama arrived at a gymnasium on Chicago's West Side, suitably named Attack Athletics. For two hours, he ran up and down the court with Senator Bob Casey, Democrat of Pennsylvania, who had become a good

America's new First Family at the victory rally in Chicago. November 4, 2008.

ABOVE: The candidate after voting in Chicago. November 4, 2008.

BELOW: The bleachers at a campaign rally at Bonanza High School in Las Vegas, Nev. October 25, 2008.

TOP RIGHT: Voters inside Chaparral High School in Parker, Colo. November 4, 2008.

friend, along with a close group of Chicago pals who were there to help take his mind off the election.

"We are all very superstitious about how things are," said Dr. Eric Whitaker, a friend who traveled with Obama for the final days of the race. "When he lost in New Hampshire and Las Vegas we didn't play, so we've not missed an election day since."

Friends tried to keep Obama, still heartbroken over the death of his grandmother two days before, surrounded by familiar Chicago faces.

By Election Day night, thousands of his admirers had gathered in Chicago's Grant Park for a victory celebration. At a nearby hotel, he took one more look at his speech, while television sets blared in the background.

Celebrities, including Oprah Winfrey, gathered in a tent to await the candidate. As Ohio was called for Obama, a roar sounded from the 125,000 people in Grant Park. It was the last state needed to give Obama enough electoral votes for victory. But the networks waited until the polls closed in California — at 11 p.m., Eastern time — before declaring Obama the winner. The candidate waited to watch McCain's gracious concession speech, in Arizona, in which

KENNETH D. LYONS/AP

McCain praised the president-elect as a fellow American and paid tribute to the fact that a black man had just been elected president.

"This is a historic election, and I recognize the significance it has for African-Americans and for the special pride that must be theirs tonight," McCain said, adding, "We both realize that we have come a long way from the injustices that once stained our nation's reputation."

Finally, looking a bit exhausted, Obama came out on the stage at Grant Park, surveying the huge crowd who had gathered to see him, waving American flags. "What a scene, what a crowd," he said, shaking his head. "Wow." He took a long drink out of the water bottle inside the lectern.

"If there is anyone out there who still doubts that America is a place where all things are possible," he said, "who still wonders if the dream of our founders is alive in our time, who still questions the power of our democracy, tonight is your answer."

"It's been a long time coming," the president-elect added, "but tonight, because of what we did on this date in this election at this defining moment, change has come to America."

"ABOVE ALL, I WILL NEVER FORGET WHO THIS VICTORY BELONGS TO— IT BELONGS TO YOU."

—BARACK OBAMA
NOVEMBER 4, 2008

MICHAEL APPLETON FOR NYT

SCOTT OLSON/GETTY IMAGES

The election scene at Grant Park in Chicago as the president-elect and his new first lady greet the crowd.

JIM YOUNG/REUTERS

DAMON WINTER/NYT

Spontaneous parties broke out on streets across America. At 2 a.m., about 20 people gathered outside The New York Times's new headquarters on Eighth Avenue, waiting for newspapers to be released. They knew the paper would be an important way to mark the historic occasion. When a senior editor appeared with a bundle of early editions of the paper, the crowd went nuts and began taking her picture holding the newspaper with the simple headline that captured their joy: OBAMA.

Oceans away in Jakarta, Indonesia, a young student attending the same public school Obama attended when he had lived there celebrated with his schoolmates. People celebrated around the world, especially in Kenya, where some members of Obama's more distant family made plans to attend the inauguration.

At Obama headquarters in Albany, Ga., Rutha Mae Harris cried tears of joy as her dream of America electing a black president came true.

"Glory, glory, hallelujah," she sang.

"IF THERE'S ANYONE OUT THERE WHO STILL DOUBTS THAT AMERICA IS A PLACE WHERE ALL THINGS ARE POSSIBLE; WHO STILL QUESTIONS THE POWER OF OUR DEMOCRACY, TONIGHT IS YOUR ANSWER."

—BARACK OBAMA
NOVEMBER 4, 2008

A woman in Grant Park, Chicago, yells, "Thank you, God!" as CNN announces that Barack Obama will become the next president of the United States. November 4, 2008.

DOUG MILLS/NYT

INSIDE THE TIMES

Planning for the election issue of The New York Times began weeks before the voting.

The political team of editors and reporters had to be ready to deal with either an Obama or McCain victory. They had assigned stories to reporters based on both outcomes, so that no matter what happened, they would have something to print the day after Election Day.

Exit polls — surveys collected as voters leave voting booths — were expected at 5 p.m. The Times's editors knew these polls would help the journalists predict the outcome of the election, but only real votes would really be able to determine what would happen.

It's hard to describe the excitement in the newsroom on election night. The third floor, where the political team and online writers and editors work, was positively humming with activity. Journalists from other parts of The Times gathered just to be near the action.

Executive Editor Bill Keller and Managing Editors Jill Abramson and John Geddes knew they were publishing a newspaper for the ages. In the event of an Obama win, they had assigned three articles for the front page, besides the main news story, which was to be written by Adam Nagourney, The Times's main political correspondent. The three articles touched on the themes of race, the enormity of the economic problems facing Obama and the new face he would show to the rest of the world.

Keller had thought of an untraditional headline: OBAMA. As the results came in and more states were being called for Obama, Abramson entered Nagourney's office to read a draft of his beautifully written story. They fiddled, just a bit, with the first sentence. Then Nagourney hit the send button:

"Barack Hussein Obama was elected the 44th president of the United States on Tuesday, sweeping away the last racial barrier in American politics with ease as the country chose him as its first black chief executive.

"The election of Mr. Obama amounted to a national catharsis — a repudiation of a historically unpopular Republican president and his economic and foreign policies, and an embrace of Mr. Obama's call for a change in the direction and the tone of the country.

"But it was just as much a strikingly symbolic moment in the evolution of the nation's fraught racial history, a breakthrough that would have seemed unthinkable just two years ago."

Once the layout of the front page had been designed and the headline chosen, Keller had one more important decision to make: the front page photograph. Michele McNally, The Times's editor of photography, brought him her two favorites, one shot by Doug Mills, another by Damon Winter. One was a close-in portrait of the president-elect at the moment of victory, the other a joyous picture of Barack, Michelle, Malia and Sasha.

Keller consulted Abramson and Geddes. Both pictures were wonderful. Mockups — layouts that show what each page would look like — of front pages with each picture were prepared and compared. Now Keller was sure: the group shot, featuring America's new first family, told the story perfectly.

Because the results were clear by 11 p.m., the editors' work was much speedier than in previous election nights. Keller, Abramson and Geddes had all been in the newsroom on election night 2000, when George W. Bush was running against Al Gore and problems with voting machines in Florida made the results uncertain. On that day, Joe Lelyveld, who was then executive editor, called out "Stop the presses!" in the very early hours of the morning when the results were still unclear. This time, there were no surprises.

The first printed papers arrived in the newsroom around 1:30 a.m. A crowd had gathered in front of the building to get the first copies. By the time the editors returned the next morning, a line had formed all the way down the block. Even though The Times had printed several hundred thousand extra papers, the entire city was sold out. More press runs were added. By Friday, when the lines began to abate, The Times had sold 25,000 election papers at its headquarters alone.

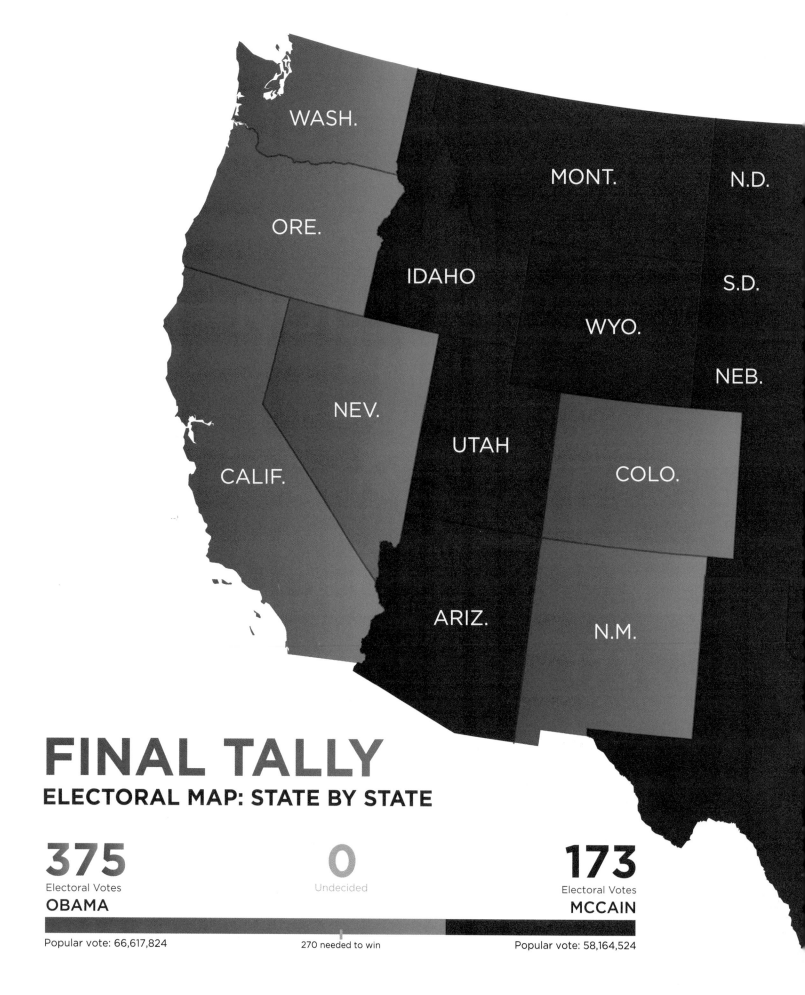

FINAL TALLY
ELECTORAL MAP: STATE BY STATE

375
Electoral Votes
OBAMA

0
Undecided

173
Electoral Votes
MCCAIN

Popular vote: 66,617,824

270 needed to win

Popular vote: 58,164,524

MINN.

WIS.

MICH.

ME.

VT.

N.H.

N.Y.

R.I.

IOWA

ILL.

IND.

OHIO

PA.

CONN.

N.J.

DEL.

D.C.

KAN.

MO.

W.V.

VA.

MD.

KY.

N.C.

OKLA.

ARK.

TENN.

S.C.

MISS.

ALA.

GA.

LA.

TEX.

FLA.

ALASKA

HAWAII

BARACK HUSSEIN OBAMA

BORN AUGUST 4, 1961 IN HONOLULU, HAWAII

RIGHTY OR LEFTY:

Left-handed

SHOE SIZE:

11

HEIGHT:

6 feet 1-1/2 inches

EDUCATION:

Occidental College
Columbia University
Harvard Law School

WIFE:

Michelle

KIDS:

Malia (born 1998)
Sasha (born 2001)

WORK EXPERIENCE:

Community Organizer
Lawyer
College Professor
Illinois State Senator
U.S. Senator

ANNUAL SALARY:

$400,000 (as President)

DOUG MILLS/NYT

ALEX BRANDON/AP

MARK LYONS FOR NYT

OZIER MUHAMMAD/NYT

OZIER MUHAMMAD/NYT

OZIER MUHAMMAD/NYT

DAMON WINTER/NYT

ALEX BRANDON/AP

DOUG MILLS/NYT

DAMON WINTER/NYT

NOTABLE FAVORITES:

BOOKS:
"Moby Dick" by Herman Melville
"Self-Reliance" by Ralph Waldo Emerson
"Song of Solomon" by Toni Morrison

MOVIES:
"Casablanca"
"Lawrence of Arabia"
"One Flew Over the Cuckoo's Nest"

MUSIC:
Bach
Miles Davis
Bob Dylan
The Fugees

TV SHOWS:
"Sportscenter"
"The Wire"

FOOD:
Chili

HOBBIES:
Basketball
Collects Spider-Man comics

HEROES:
Mohandas Gandhi
Martin Luther King Jr.
Pablo Picasso

TIME OF
TRANSITION

The financial crisis was reaching such desperate levels that almost every large institution, from investment banks to insurers, was approaching Washington for money. Help couldn't wait. People were losing their jobs. Many were in danger of losing their homes, unable to afford their mortgages.

Although Barack Obama kept reminding people that the United States only had one president at a time — and he wouldn't officially take office until his inauguration on Jan. 20, 2009 — he knew the world expected him to help stabilize the financial system. That meant the quick announcement of an economic team and a financial plan to boost the economy, perhaps one involving as much as $700 billion in government money, equivalent to the financial bailout plan already approved by the Congress before the election.

President-elect Obama and President Bush walk to the Oval Office during the Obamas' first official visit to the White House. November 10, 2008.

In the Democrats' weekly radio address in late November, Obama said he would direct his economic team to design a two-year plan with the goal of saving or creating 2.5 million jobs. "The news this week has only reinforced the fact that we are facing an economic crisis of historic proportions," he said.

The crisis seemed to weaken the battle lines between Democrats — who tend to favor tax increases to pay for additional government services — and Republicans — who usually support lower taxes and fewer government programs. Obama, for his part, agreed that raising taxes, even on the wealthiest Americans, was probably not a good idea in the current climate. The issue was one that he and John McCain had argued about during the debates, with McCain against any tax increases and Obama supporting them for the richest Americans, those earning more than $250,000 a year. Republicans, meanwhile, agreed that government spending was now necessary to jump-start the economy.

Even before Obama had finished announcing his cabinet, the automotive companies — G.M., Chrysler and Ford — were in Washington asking for billions in loans to prevent bankruptcy and eventual failure.

President-elect Obama takes questions during his first press conference after the election, Chicago. November 7, 2008.

PHOTOS: DOUG MILLS/NYT

The Obamas meet the Bushes at the White House, getting a tour of their future home. November 10, 2008.

"I DON'T THINK YOU SHOULD SETTLE FOR A PRESIDENT WHO'S ONLY THERE FOR YOU WHEN IT'S EASY OR CONVENIENT OR POPULAR; I THINK YOU DESERVE A PRESIDENT WHO'S WILLING TO FIGHT FOR YOU EVERY HOUR OF EVERY DAY FOR THE NEXT FOUR YEARS."

—BARACK OBAMA
NOVEMBER 3, 2007

For his first staff announcements, the president-elect turned to Representative Rahm Emanuel of Illinois as his chief of staff and John Podesta to help his transition. Both were respected for their effectiveness and Washington knowledge.

For his new Treasury secretary, Obama chose Timothy F. Geithner, the young president of the Federal Reserve Bank of New York. News of his appointment helped send the stock market up by nearly 500 points after days of sharp losses. Former Treasury Secretary Lawrence H. Summers was to be the director of the National Economic Council in the White House, the president's main economic adviser and policy coordinator. Both men believed in free trade, deregulation (removing government restrictions from economic dealings) and financial discipline.

For his national security team, Obama also chose politicians with experience. The biggest surprise was Hillary Rodham Clinton for secretary of state. Although she and Obama disagreed about the Iraq war and battled fiercely during the Democratic primary races, Clinton accepted the appointment. From the

> "THERE'S A CERTAIN TONE IN POLITICS I ASPIRE TO THAT ALLOWS ME TO DISAGREE WITH PEOPLE WITHOUT BEING DISAGREEABLE."
>
> —BARACK OBAMA
> JUNE 4, 2004

TOP LEFT: Obama asked to meet with all the living presidents at the White House. From left: George H.W. Bush, Barack Obama, George W. Bush, Bill Clinton and Jimmy Carter. January 7, 2009.

BOTTOM LEFT: Obama with his choice for secretary of state: his former opponent, New York Senator Hillary Rodham Clinton. December 1, 2008.

first news that she had met with the president-elect in Chicago to the announcement of her appointment on Dec. 1, the media leapt at the opportunity to see a revival of the Hillary-Barack duel.

Obama asked Bush's defense secretary, Robert M. Gates, to stay on, and picked Gen. James L. Jones, the former NATO commander and Marine Corps commandant, to be national security adviser. Another former rival for the Democratic nomination, Bill Richardson of New Mexico, was chosen for Commerce secretary, but later withdrew. Arizona's Janet Napolitano was selected as secretary of Homeland Security. All were expected to be approved by Congress.

The pace of appointments was much faster than usual and the many experienced appointees suggested that the new president was aware that he had no time for experimentation or mistakes. The bloody November 2008 terrorist attacks in Mumbai, India, deepening instability in Pakistan and Afghanistan and periodic flare-ups in Iraq gave new meaning to the "fierce urgency of now."

ABOVE: During a meeting at his transition office in Washington. January 6, 2009.

BELOW: The president-elect stops for chili in his new hometown, Washington, D.C. January 10, 2009.

POOL PHOTO BY KENT NISHIMURA

Historians made comparisons to previous presidents who came to power during times of turmoil, such as Lincoln, who took office at the beginning of the Civil War, and Roosevelt, who faced the Depression in the '30s.

Although his campaign nickname was "No Drama Obama," his choices meant an Obama White House that would have many big personalities and far more debate than occurred among the team President George W. Bush picked during his first term.

The staff also included campaign hands like David Axelrod and Robert Gibbs, the press secretary, and old Chicago friends like Valerie Jarrett. Jarrett and White House Social Secretary Desiree Rogers were put in charge of keeping the Obamas' Chicago friends connected to the First Couple.

With so many new responsibilities, Obama had little time for post-election relaxation, although he visited the gym in Chicago for nearly 90 minutes every day. Over the Christmas holiday, the Obamas took a vacation in Hawaii, where the president-elect indulged his passion for golf. But there was sad family business awaiting them: scattering Toot's ashes near the spot where Barack had scattered those of his mother.

Obama asked to meet with all of the living presidents to seek advice. In January, President Bush hosted a White House luncheon for the group, which included Jimmy Carter, George H.W. Bush and Bill Clinton.

The Obamas moved out of their house in Chicago and into a suite at the Hay-Adams Hotel, near the White House, so that Malia and Sasha could begin school after the holiday break. Besides a few official photographs of the president-elect seeing the girls off to school, the press gave Malia and Sasha the privacy to adjust and make new friends at Sidwell Friends.

There was one more announcement before the family moved into the White House: Marian Robinson, Michelle's mother and a mainstay for the girls all through the campaign, said she would move in with the First Family after all. And the closely followed saga of which breed of dog would share the Obama White House narrowed to two: Labradoodle and Portuguese water dog.

At the Democratic Convention in Denver. August 25, 2008.

ROBYN BECK/AFP/GETTY IMAGES

ALEX BRANDON/AP

THE NEW FIRST DAUGHTERS

During Barack Obama's first news conference after the election, the most pressing question was about what kind of puppy the Obamas planned to get in the White House, a promise they had made to their daughters, Malia (pronounced Muh-LEE-ah), 10, and Sasha, 7. Next, the frenzy turned to what school the girls would attend in Washington.

Michelle looked at several private schools and chose Sidwell Friends, a nurturing Quaker school that had educated Chelsea Clinton, Al Gore's son and many other children of politicians.

Every member of the first family receives a code name from the Secret Service and the girls would be known as Rosebud and Radiance. They would be the youngest children to live in the White House since the Kennedys. Happy talk about White House sleepovers during an interview on "60 Minutes" did little to hide the Obamas' worries over moving their young daughters into the center of First Family mania. They didn't want all the media attention to upset Malia and Sasha.

Michelle told friends she wanted the girls to have as normal a routine as possible. While the White House staff could make her bed, she wanted the girls to make their own.

Michelle also said she intended to be more of a "mom-in-chief" than first lady and picked as her signature issue helping military families.

Obama was a protective father who never missed a parent-teacher conference. He read Harry Potter with Malia and roughhoused with Sasha. In her convention speech, Michelle recalled him

MARCO GARCÍA/AP

DOUG MILLS/NYT

MARCO GARCÍA/AP

From left, walking on the beach with Dad and adjusting a flower in Malia's ear during an August 2008 vacation in Hawaii; a kiss for Sasha during a November rally in Springfield, Mo.; and horsing around in Fort Wayne, Ind., in May.

driving home with her and baby Malia so slowly, with so many backward glances at the infant in the back seat, that she feared they would never make it home. It was obvious he took the responsibility of fatherhood quite seriously.

Michelle's mother, Marian, 71, who had helped care for the girls while she campaigned, would be moving into the White House as well.

On "60 Minutes" Obama called the possibility of disrupting their lives "one of my greatest worries." For the most part, the Obamas had protected the girls during the campaign. The public saw only traditional photos of the girls at the convention and on election night, followed by a few shots of the family on vacation in Hawaii and moving to Washington. Barack and Michelle wanted to keep their daughters' lives as private as possible. "If at the end of four years, just from a personal standpoint, we can say they are who they are — they remain the great joys that they are — and this hasn't created a whole bunch of problems for them, then I think we're going to feel pretty good," he said.

DOUG MILLS/NYT

The Presidential Inaugural Committee

requests the honor of your presence

to attend and participate

in the

Inauguration of

Barack H. Obama

as President of the United States of America

and

Joseph R. Biden, Jr.

as Vice President of the United States of America

on Tuesday, the twentieth of January

two thousand and nine

in the City of Washington

PRESIDENT
OBAMA

The weekend before the inauguration, President-elect Barack Obama and his family had stopped to visit the Lincoln Memorial, studying the words carved into the marble. Considering his inaugural speech, ten-year-old Malia turned to her father and advised, "First African-American president. Better be good."

Although Obama would not become president until noon on Jan. 20, 2009, the inaugural celebration began at 11:30 a.m. on Jan. 17, on a blue train car traveling from Philadelphia to Washington, a shorter version of President Abraham Lincoln's famous journey in 1861. Michelle Obama, who turned 45 that day, danced in the aisles with Malia, Sasha and some friends. They picked up Vice President-elect Joseph R. Biden Jr. and his wife, Jill, in Wilmington, Del.

The day before moving into the White House, the Obamas observed a national day of service on the birthday of Dr. Martin Luther King Jr. As he painted the walls of a shelter for teenagers in Washington, D.C., one of the shelter workers asked Obama if he was sweating.

"Nah, I don't sweat," the president-elect replied.

On Inauguration Day, as the Obamas and the Bushes headed to the swearing-in ceremony, the White House staff packed the belongings of the Bush family and unpacked the Obamas'. The quick change was accomplished without a single mover setting foot inside 1600 Pennsylvania Avenue (the president's official address). Craig Robinson, Michelle's brother, had jokingly asked her how many bathrooms the White House had. (The answer: 34.)

ABOVE: Barack Obama paints the walls at Sasha Bruce Youthwork Center in Washington, D.C. January 19, 2009.

BELOW: President-elect Obama arrives at his inauguration, Washington, D.C. January 20, 2009.

Obama took the oath of office on the west front of the U.S. Capitol. He gave his inaugural address a few minutes after noon, looking out at close to two million people who had gathered across the National Mall, all the way to the Lincoln Memorial. Many of the people who braved the 17-degree weather said they would not believe America would install a black president until they saw and heard him sworn in.

A crowd of diverse Americans cheered and cried as Obama took his oath of office. Then he gave an 18-minute inaugural address, which expressed his hope for the future but also served as a serious reminder to Americans that everyone's help was needed to turn things around. The economic crisis was worsening, and the U.S. was still involved in two wars abroad.

After he was done, his 7-year-old daughter Sasha told him: "That was a pretty good speech, Dad."

Obama became emotional when the Rev. Joseph E. Lowery, an important figure of the civil rights movement, gave the closing prayer and preached for "inclusion, not exclusion, tolerance, not intolerance."

After the new president's inaugural address, former President Bush left for his home in Texas. He

"ON THIS DAY, WE GATHER BECAUSE WE HAVE CHOSEN HOPE OVER FEAR, UNITY OF PURPOSE OVER CONFLICT AND DISCORD."

—BARACK OBAMA
JANUARY 20, 2009

ABOVE: President Obama used Abraham Lincoln's inaugural Bible. January 20, 2009.

LEFT: Taking the oath, administered by Chief Justice John G. Roberts Jr. January 20, 2009.

"THE QUESTION WE ASK TODAY IS NOT WHETHER OUR GOVERNMENT IS TOO BIG OR TOO SMALL, BUT WHETHER IT WORKS — WHETHER IT HELPS FAMILIES FIND JOBS AT A DECENT WAGE, CARE THEY CAN AFFORD, A RETIREMENT THAT IS DIGNIFIED."

—BARACK OBAMA
JANUARY 20, 2009

The new president gives his inaugural address, Washington, D.C. January 20, 2009.

hugged Obama, then headed out through the rotunda of the Capitol. "Come on, Laura, we're going home," he was overheard telling the former first lady.

On the streets of Washington, strangers hugged one another. Many could no longer feel their feet because of the cold, but there was joyful dancing anyway.

Across the country and around the world, there were equally jubilant displays. In Kisumu, Kenya, people stood atop their bicycles to watch the inaugural party celebrating the son of their former countryman becoming the new American president. Iraqis gathered in cafes in Baghdad to watch the televised coverage, while American soldiers exchanged high fives at a base in Kabul.

Along the inaugural parade route, tens of thousands huddled in the cold to catch a glimpse of the new president. The Obamas got out of their car and walked for several minutes, holding hands and beaming. One of the bands had a special place in the new president's heart, the Punahou School band from Hawaii, where Obama had graduated.

After the parade, the first couple went back to the White House to change for a big night of parties. While Malia and Sasha watched movies in their new home, the Obamas left for 10 inaugural balls, he in a new tuxedo and white bow tie, she in a gown made of ivory silk chiffon.

For their first dance Beyoncé sang "At Last." At one of their stops, the president asked the crowd, "First of all, how good-looking is my wife?"

There was much to celebrate, but in a few hours, he would begin his first full day of work in the Oval Office, ready to meet the challenges facing the country.

DOUG MILLS/NYT

DAMON WINTER/NYT

★ ★ ★ ★ ★ ★ ★

> "FOR WE KNOW THAT OUR PATCH-WORK HERITAGE IS A STRENGTH, NOT A WEAKNESS. WE ARE A NATION OF CHRISTIANS AND MUSLIMS, JEWS AND HINDUS — AND NON-BELIEVERS. WE ARE SHAPED BY EVERY LANGUAGE AND CULTURE, DRAWN FROM EVERY END OF THIS EARTH."
>
> —BARACK OBAMA
> JANUARY 20, 2009

TOP LEFT: *The crowd on the National Mall erupts into cheers after President Barack Obama finishes his oath of office. January 20, 2009.*

TOP RIGHT: *A thumb's up on the inaugural address from daughter Sasha. January 20, 2009.*

LEFT: *Cheers at the Youth Ball. January 20, 2009.*

RIGHT: *The couple's first dance at the Neighborhood Ball, where Beyoncé sang to them. January 20, 2009.*

JENNIFER MUÑOZ, AGE 10

DEAR SIR OBAMA: PRESIDENTIAL ADVICE

Every day after school about 65 kids, mostly middle-schoolers from Latino homes, come into 826 Valencia — a nonprofit literacy center in San Francisco — to get help with their homework. The place is always vibrant, but on November 5, 2008, it was especially so. The election of Barack Obama had made a big impact on the kids of 826 Valencia.

While the kids celebrated Obama's election, we had an idea: to ask them to express their thoughts to their new president in personalized letters.

Our sister 826 National chapters — located in New York, Chicago, Los Angeles, Michigan, Boston and Seattle — also asked their students to write letters. The resulting letters contained hilarious advice, unusual questions or heartfelt pleas for a better life. Almost all of them identified with Sasha and Malia. One student, Ribika Hailemariam, born in Ethiopia, even offered advice on moving to a new town.

These kids have a way of getting to the heart of matters honestly and bluntly. As Sheenie Shannon Yip, a 13-year-old from Seattle, wrote to the new president, "I really hope you put America back together. No pressure, though."

—Jory John, Program Director

FROM THE BOOK "THANKS AND HAVE FUN RUNNING THE COUNTRY: KIDS' LETTERS TO PRESIDENT OBAMA," PUBLISHED BY MCSWEENEY'S, FEBRUARY 2009

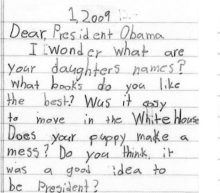

ALEJANDRA MEDINA,
AGE 8

DEAN LANCASTER,
AGE 12

MICHELLE BENITEZ,
AGE 7

ADRIAN PEREZ,
AGE 11

JINHEE JUNG,
AGE 9

NATALIE ROSALES,
AGE 6

Dear Barack Obama,
you look too skinny
you should eat more food
this is what you should eat:

1. pizza
2. iccream
3. Butter popcorn
4. cupcakes
5. Hamburgers
6. french fries
7. Hot dogs
8. hot chocolate
9. cookies
10. cotton candy

from,
Jayme

1, 2009
Dear, President Obama
I I wonder what are
your daughters names?
What books do you like
the best? Wus it easy
to move in the White House
Does your puppy make a
mess? Do you think it
was a good idea to
be President?

I hope you like the
White House??

From:Karina Aldana

dear Barack
Obama,
I,m glad
your'e
I cool.
good LUCK.

from,
Juan

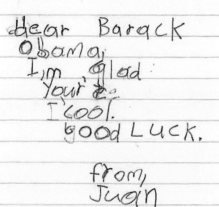

MARTHA SANCHEZ,
AGE 8

JAZMARY RIVERA,
AGE 12

KARINA ALDANA,
AGE 8

CHRISTIAN CRUZ,
AGE 7

ALEJANDRA SANCHEZ,
AGE 8

RENEA HARRIS-PETERSON,
AGE 9

COURTESY OF OBAMA FOR AMERICA

LANE TURNER/BOSTON GLOBE

DAMON WINTER/NYT

JIM YOUNG/REUTERS

MARK WILSON/GETTY IMAGES

TODD HEISLER/NYT

CLOCKWISE FROM TOP LEFT:
Barack as a toddler; as a Harvard
Law School student; at the Democratic
National Convention; with four former
presidents; election night excitement in
Chicago; and at a rally in Reno, Nev.

THESE PHOTOGRAPHS ARE USED IN COLLAGE FORM ON PAGES 8-9

ACKNOWLEDGMENTS

JILL ABRAMSON is the author of this narrative, but she has constructed it on behalf of The Times and in collaboration with colleagues who covered every step of the presidential campaign. Parts of her narrative are based on a series of biographical profiles The Times published under the collective title "The Long Run." In writing the text, Abramson drew freely from the analysis, reporting, ideas and verbatim phrases already published in The Times, as well as from her own impressions drawn from editing and reporting during the long campaign season. It would be hard to improve on the prose of Jodi Kantor, Janny Scott, Adam Nagourney or Kevin Sack, to cite but a few examples, so she has often not even tried. Because so much of the text comes by design from work that previously appeared in The Times, citations to specific articles are not included. Sources used from outside of The Times are attributed.

The Times's coverage of the election was a team effort, combining the talents of the most insightful and dedicated journalists ever to grace our profession. Every page of this book reflects their superlative work.

With our thanks and awe:

Michele V. Agins, David Ahntholz, Monica Almeida, Josh Anderson, Peter Baker, Noma Bar, James Edward Bates, Jo Becker, Keith Bedford, Rob Bennett, Barry Blitt, Julie Bosman, Isaac Brekken, John Broder, David Brooks, Nathaniel Brooks, Elisabeth Bumiller, Jackie Calme, André Carrilho, Rina Castelnuovo, Roger Cohen, Gail Collins, Marjorie Connelly, Fred R. Conrad, Fabrizio Constantini, Michael Cooper, Rebecca Corbett, Andrew Councill, Monica Davey, Beatrice DeGea, Maureen Dowd, Chris Drew, Janet Elder, Sarah Elliott, Jonathan Ellis, Matt Ericcson, James Estrin, Susan Etheridge, Shepard Fairey, Michael Falcone, Beth Flynn, Ruth Fremson, Thomas L. Friedman, Jeffrey Gettleman, Mary Ann Giordano, David Goldman, Michael Gordon, Josh Haner, John Harwood, Patrick Healy, Todd Heisler, Andrew Henderson, Bob Herbert, Ray Hernandez, David Herszenhorn, Tyler Hicks, Jodi Hilton, Evelyn Hockstein, Farhana Hossain, Carl Hulse, Erik Jacobs, Erik T. Johnson, Nadav Kander, Jodi Kantor, Kurt Kauper, David Kirkpatrick, Jessica Kourkounis, Nicholas D. Kristof, Paul Krugman, Jeremy Lange, Chang W. Lee, Mark Leibovich, David Leonhardt, Erik S. Lesser, Chip Litherland, Jim Lo Scalzo, John Loomis, Meaghan Looram, Joshua Lott, Veronika Lukasova, Michael Luo, Mark Lyons, Hiroko Masuike, Thom McGuire, Mike McIntire, Michele McNally, Doug Mills, Yan Pei-Ming, Kevin Moloney, Ozier Muhammad, Gerry Mullany, Michael Nagle, Adam Nagourney, Christoph Niemann, Merrill Oliver, Louie Palu, Ashley Parker, Yana Paskova, Sergio Peçanha, Richard Perry, Elizabeth Peyton, Kate Phillips, Michael Powell, Gina Privitere, Matt Purdy, Ramin Rahimian, Frank Rich, Larry Rohter, Jim Rutenberg, Sally Ryan, Kevin Sack, Moises Saman, David E. Sanger, Susan Saulny, Stephen Savage, Cornelius Schmid, Janny Scott, Kit Seelye, Cheryl Senter, Magdalena Sharpe, Jacob Silberberg, Brendan Smialowski, Jennifer Steinhauer, Dick Stevenson, Robert Stolarik, Sheryl Gay Stolberg, Michael Stravato, Dalia Sussman, Rachel Swarns, Jeff Swenson, Casey Templeton, Eric Thayer, Megan Thee, Robin Toner, Lisa Tozzi, Archie Tse, Don Van Natta, Dilip Vishwanat, Kara Walker, Leslie Wayne, Nancy Weinstock, Ben Werschkul, Sarah Wheaton, Max Whittaker, Jim Wilson, Damon Winter, Caroline Yang, Jeff Zeleny, Kate Zernike

Grateful thanks to Steve Crowley and Dave Scull, whose early eyes on this project made all the difference.

Special thanks: Matt Bai, Nicholas Blechman, Tom Bodkin, Phyllis Collazo, Theresa Derosa, Steve Duenes, Tomi Murata, Merrill Perlman, Jeff Roth, Kathy Ryan, Bill Stockland, the photographers of the agencies and wire services, Dan Pfeiffer, and the Obama family and transition team

Satellite photo of the National Mall in Washington, D.C., during the inauguration of Barack Obama. January 20, 2009.

GEOEYE/AFP/GETTY IMAGES

THE WHITE HOUSE

First day in the Oval Office.
January 21, 2009.

The New York Times

CALLAWAY

Nicholas Callaway wishes to thank the following artists and representatives for their generosity:
Charles Buchan, Mo Cohen, Dave Eggers, Jory John, Scott Moyers, Pete Souza, and Andrew Wylie.

Printed in the U.S.A.

DISTRIBUTED BY VIKING CHILDREN'S BOOKS, A DIVISION OF PENGUIN YOUNG READERS GROUP

First Edition
10 9 8 7 6 5 4 3 2 1

Library of Congress Cataloging-in-Publication Data available.

ISBN 978-0-670-01208-4

Visit The New York Times at www.nytimes.com   Visit Callaway at www.callaway.com

Produced by CALLAWAY ARTS & ENTERTAINMENT
19 FULTON STREET, FIFTH FLOOR, NEW YORK, NY 10038

Nicholas Callaway, President and Publisher · John Lee, CEO · Cathy Ferrara, Managing Editor and Production Director
Toshiya Masuda, Art Director · Nelson Gómez, Director of Digital Technology · Amy Cloud, Senior Editor
Krupa Jhaveri, Designer · Bomina Kim, Design Assistant · Ivan Wong, Jr. and Jose Rodriguez, Production
Jennifer Caffrey, Executive Assistant